Ortho Easy-Step Books

Decks

*Created and designed
by the editorial staff of
Ortho Books*

Contents

Easy Steps to a New Deck

A deck can add living space to your home at a fraction of the cost of an addition. Many people find that when the weather is beautiful, they do all their entertaining outdoors. It's just a great place to relax. In addition to the enjoyment it provides, a carefully designed and well-built deck will increase the value of your home. And a deck can be fun to build. A homeowner with basic construction skills can do the job quickly—often over a couple of weekends. And such fast results add to the pleasure of improving your home.

Decks is a one-stop guide to helping you do a professional-looking job at sweat-equity savings. If this is your first major carpentry project, don't panic. Even skilled carpenters make mistakes—but they know how to correct them. The construction stages in *Decks* are made as correctable as possible. You'll find that a framing member out of plumb or the slight misplacement of a post can be fixed in a later step. And although you should be comfortable using such carpentry tools as a circular saw and power drill, the straightforward design requires no special cuts or joints—just basic skills and the tools found in most home workshops.

This book shows you how to build a simple rectangular deck adaptable to almost any site. Options in decking and railing design let you choose a style that best suits your house. Special attention has been paid to fastening techniques that limit the chance for water damage. So whether you use heart redwood or plain, pressure-treated pine, you can be confident that your approach will prolong the life of the structure and let you enjoy your new living space for many years to come.

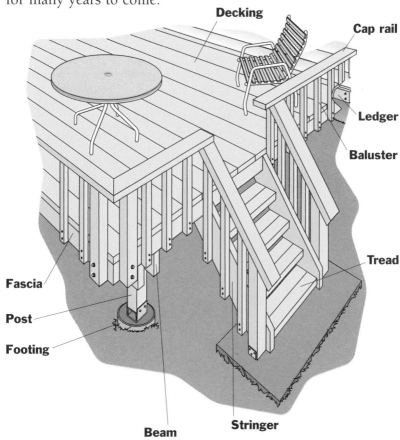

Decking

Cap rail

Ledger

Baluster

Tread

Fascia

Post

Footing

Beam

Stringer

1 Plan the location

Draw a site plan of your home and yard that includes all doors, windows, utility hookups, fences, walks, trees, and shrubs. Note the sun/shade patterns and how they change during the day and from season to season. Include everything that might affect the deck location, such as setbacks, wind, downspouts, septic tank, and underground utility lines. Next, overlay tracing paper and sketch possible locations. Consider proximity to the house—especially the kitchen or family room—deck size and shape, access to the garden, views, privacy, sun, shade, and wind.

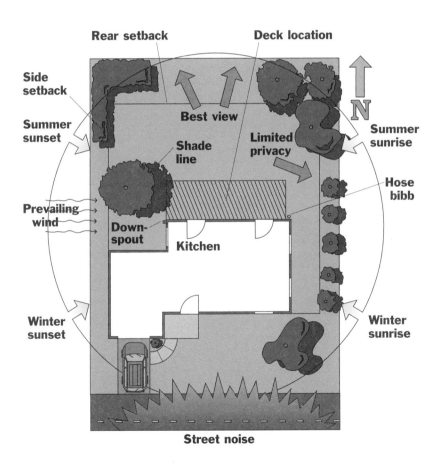

Draw the plans

At a scale of ¼ or ½ inch per foot, draw the deck outline and direction of the decking boards. Also draw a framing and foundation plan. It should include joists, ledger, beam or stringers, posts, concrete footings, stair framing, and blocking. Then, using the same scale, draw elevations that show side views of the deck and railings in relation to the house and ground. Finally, make enlarged detail sketches that show the dimensions, hardware, and fastening methods for the footings, ledger, stairs, and railings.

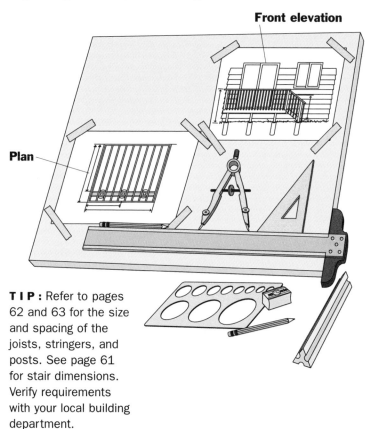

Front elevation

Plan

TIP: Refer to pages 62 and 63 for the size and spacing of the joists, stringers, and posts. See page 61 for stair dimensions. Verify requirements with your local building department.

To get a good sense of how much additional living space the deck will provide, use flour, rope, or a garden hose to mark the proposed perimeter. Take into account deck furniture, planters, and barbecue equipment—you might even want to set some of these items in place. Check to see that traffic flow is adequate, being especially careful to situate the stairs so that house-to-yard traffic is direct without interfering with seating areas on the deck. If the deck is not at the same floor level as the house, plan a large landing, avoiding steps directly outside the doorway.

Deck furniture

Garden hose

Make a materials list

Use the following checklist, your plans, and the information in this book to make a materials list. Keep in mind that lumber is sold in even 2-foot increments—you can buy a 10-foot 2×6, for example, but not an 11-foot one. Also, lumber dimensions are not quite what they seem. For example, "2-by" lumber is actually about 1½ inches thick; "1-by" lumber is ¾ inch thick. Decking called "five-quarter" is sometimes the full 1¼ inches thick and sometimes 1 inch. See page 58 for information about deck lumber.

Footings
- Concrete
- Forming tubes
- Gravel for the bottom of footing holes
- Rebar

Structural lumber
(see the span tables on pages 62 and 63)
- 4×4s for posts
- 4-bys or double 2-bys for beams
- 2-bys for ledger, joists, header, and blocking

Decking
- 2×4, 2×6, or ⁵⁄₄ decking

Stairs
- 2×12s for stringers
- 2×6s for treads

Railings
- 4×4s for posts
- 2×4s for top rail
- ⁵⁄₄ decking or 2×6 for cap rail
- 2×2s or 1×3s for balusters
- 1-bys for fascia

Hardware
- J-bolts for post anchors
- Post anchors for footings
- Beam connectors
- Flashing for ledger
- Angle brackets for joists and stringers
- Joist hangers for interior joists
- Tread cleats for stairs

Fasteners
- ⅜-inch by 4½-inch lag screws with washers
- Spacers or extra washers for attaching ledger
- Joist-hanger nails
- Bolts, nuts, and washers for assembling the beam
- Decking screws and/or nails for decking and railings
- Lag screws for attaching stair treads
- Duplex nails for forms and temporary bracing

Finishing
- Caulk
- Sealer
- Stain

Organize your tools

A typical deck-building project requires the tools shown below. Although not essential, other tools that might be helpful are a chop saw (power miter saw), reciprocating saw, belt sander, adjustable clamps, and hoe. Use gloves when digging or handling lumber. If you use pressure-treated lumber, carefully note the manufacturer's warnings about protection from dust while sawing. When using power tools, plug the cords into a receptacle protected by a ground fault circuit interrupter (GFCI).

1

Prepare the site

The deck won't protect the ground under it from rainwater, so make sure water will drain away from the house. Some of the ground under the deck can be soggy at times, but the areas around the footings must be firm. If the deck won't be raised much above ground, smooth high spots with a rake or shovel. To ensure that nothing will grow under the deck, cover the area first with two layers of black plastic sheeting. Punch holes every square foot or so to allow for drainage. Then cover the plastic with a layer of gravel.

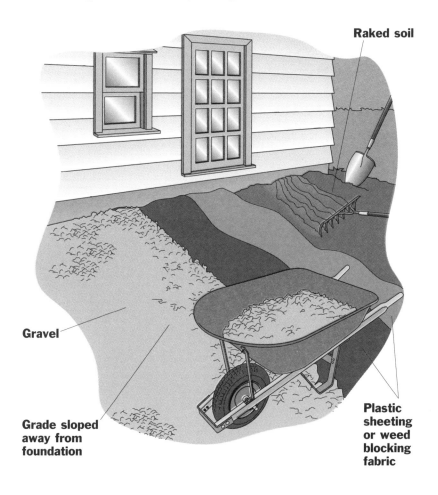

Raked soil

Gravel

Grade sloped away from foundation

Plastic sheeting or weed blocking fabric

2 Locate the ledger

The ledger is the point of reference for the whole deck, so place it carefully. Cut the ledger 4½ inches shorter than the finished deck (for the 1½-inch joist and ¾-inch fascia that will be added to each end of the ledger). Position the top of the ledger 2½ inches below the house floor—2 inches if you use ⁵⁄₄-inch decking. Tack or prop the ledger in place temporarily, and double-check that it is level.

TIP: If your house siding is not level, a level deck may look odd in relation to it. This can be avoided by positioning the ledger as far as possible below the lower edge of a siding board. You may even want to loosen a course or two of siding directly above the ledger and renail it parallel to the deck.

Deck surface will be 1", 1¼", or 1½" above top of ledger, depending on thickness of decking boards.

3

Drill the ledger

Drill through the ledger with a ¼-inch bit so the bit makes shallow holes in the siding. Place two holes every 24 inches. Then remove the ledger. If the screws will be going through siding and wood framing, complete the drilling with the same ¼-inch bit. You will be drilling into the header joist of your home's floor framing—a strong support for the deck. If you are attaching to masonry or concrete, use a masonry bit to bore holes for expansion bolts. Insert the anchors into the holes before attaching the ledger.

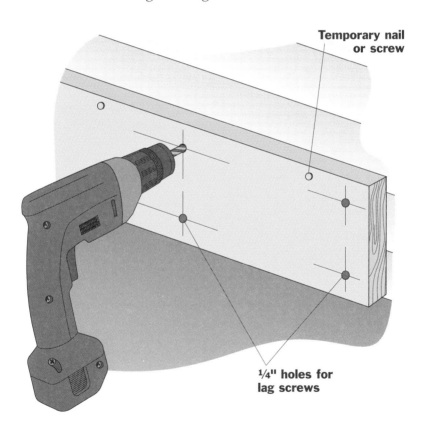

Temporary nail or screw

¼" holes for lag screws

Install the ledger

To ensure that water will not get trapped between the ledger and siding, use spacers when installing the ledger. For the spacers, use 10 or 12 washers, cut ¾-inch sections from aluminum pipe, or buy aluminum or plastic spacers. Don't tighten the lag screws until all screws and spacers have been started into their holes. First tighten one screw at one end of the ledger. Then recheck for level before tightening the screws on the opposite end. Once the ledger is level, tighten all the screws.

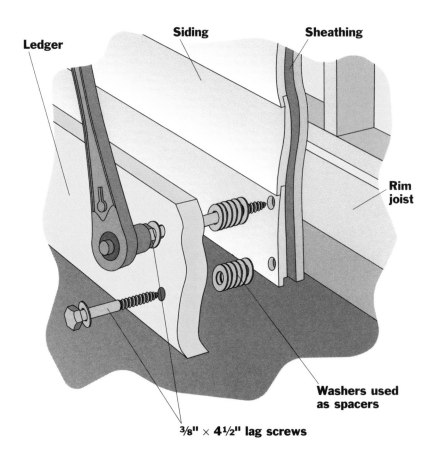

Siding

Sheathing

Ledger

Rim joist

Washers used as spacers

⅜" × 4½" lag screws

Build batter boards

For layout, build two pairs of batter boards. Use 3-foot 2×4s for the stakes and crosspieces; trim the stakes to a point. Drive each pair of stakes into the ground about 3 feet behind the approximate location of the corner footings. Using a water level, make reference marks on all the stakes and the house wall at the ledger. At the wall, measure the vertical distance from the mark to the top of the ledger. Use this measurement on each stake to show where the top of the crosspiece should go, then screw or nail the crosspiece to the stakes.

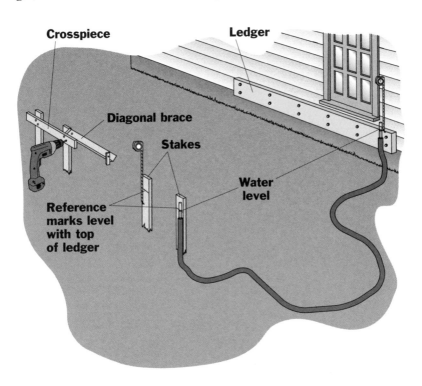

Crosspiece

Ledger

Diagonal brace

Stakes

Water level

Reference marks level with top of ledger

Lay out string lines

Tack two nails into the top of the ledger. Find these points by measuring in from the ends of the ledger the same distance that the posts will be centered from the ends of the beam—less 1½ inches for each side joist. Tie strings to the nails.

While a helper stretches the strings to the batter boards, use a framing square to check that each string is roughly square to the ledger. If necessary, adjust the strings, then secure them. Lay out a third string line across the back where the posts will be centered.

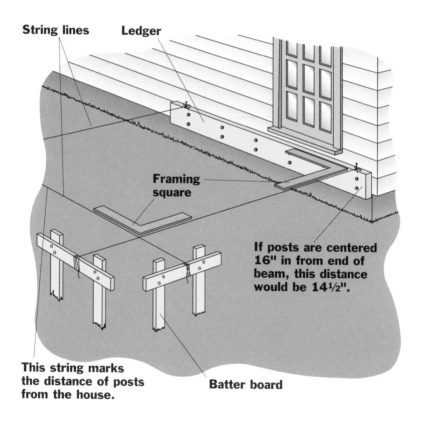

String lines   **Ledger**

Framing square

If posts are centered 16" in from end of beam, this distance would be 14½".

This string marks the distance of posts from the house.

Batter board

Check for square

To check corners, use the "3-4-5" method: Mark a point on the ledger 3 feet from the string, and a point on the string 4 feet from the ledger. Measure the distance between the two marks. If it is exactly 5 feet, the corner is square. For greater accuracy, use 6, 8, and 10 feet, or 9, 12, and 15. To check all four corners, simply measure the diagonals. If they are equal, the layout is square. Once all is square, drive a nail into each batter board where the string crosses it and tie the string to the nail.

Diagonal measurements should be equal.

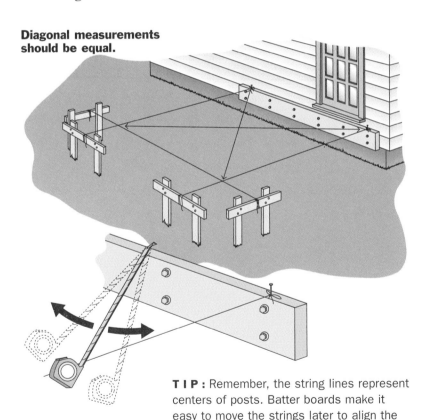

T I P : Remember, the string lines represent centers of posts. Batter boards make it easy to move the strings later to align the edges of the posts, and later again to align the edges of the deck.

Installing the Footings

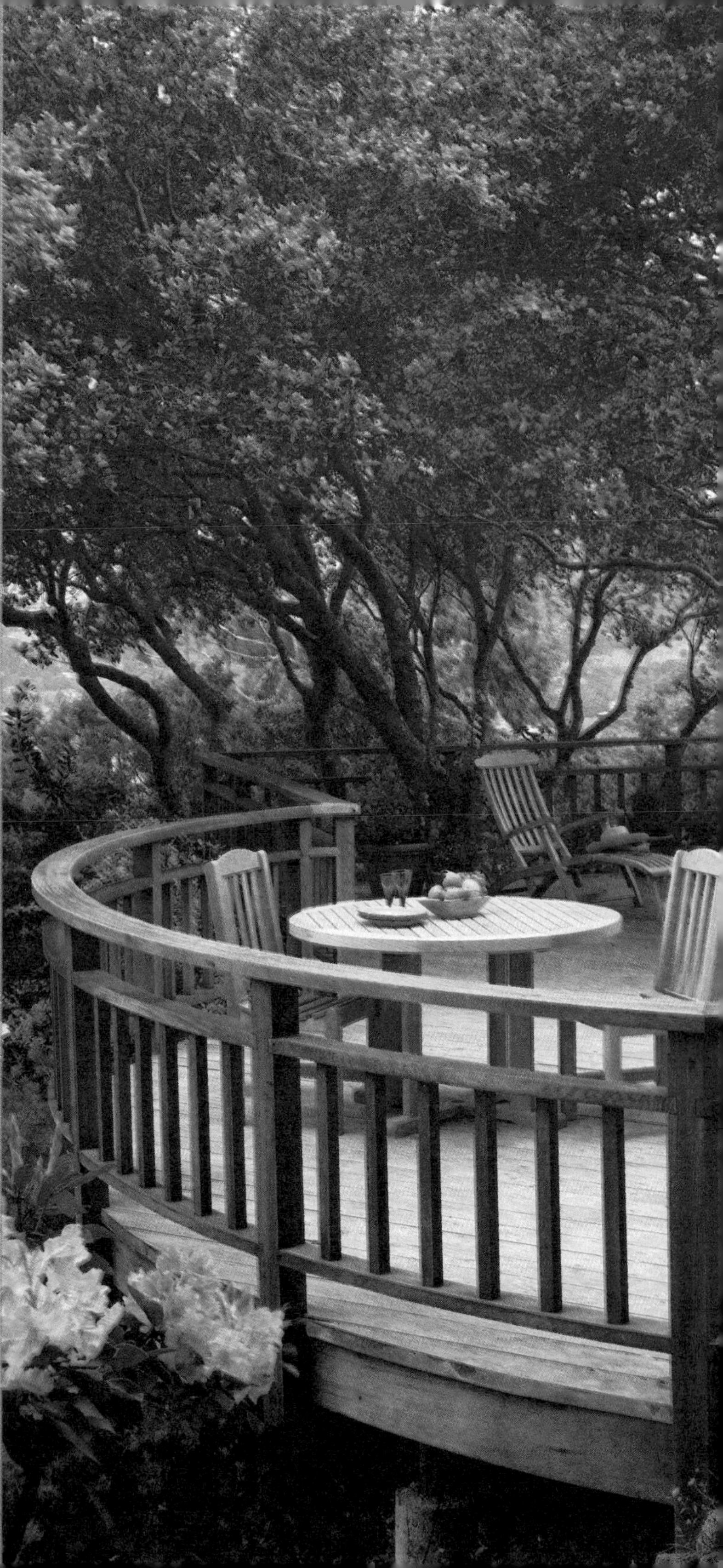

1 Mark for footings

Using a plumb bob or chalk-line reel, find the point on the ground directly below each string-line intersection and mark it with a nail or small stake. These points represent the centers of the corner posts. For intermediate posts, measure along the string line and mark it with tape. Then plumb down from these marks and place nails or stakes to indicate the centers of posts.

Using the nails for reference, measure and mark footing outlines on the ground with flour or chalk. Shallow footings are 18 inches square; deep footings are 10 to 12 inches round.

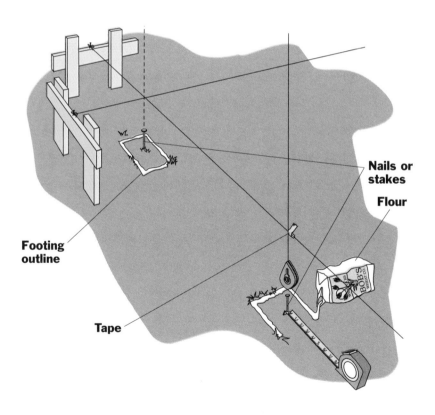

Nails or stakes

Flour

Footing outline

Tape

Dig the holes

Consult your local building department to determine how deep the footings must be. Keep the bottom level, and the sides of the holes as straight as possible. If you have a lot of holes to dig, or if they must be more than 3 feet deep, do yourself a favor and rent a power auger. Flare the bottom of deep holes with a trenching shovel or posthole digger to widen the footing base. This will "key" the footing into the ground.

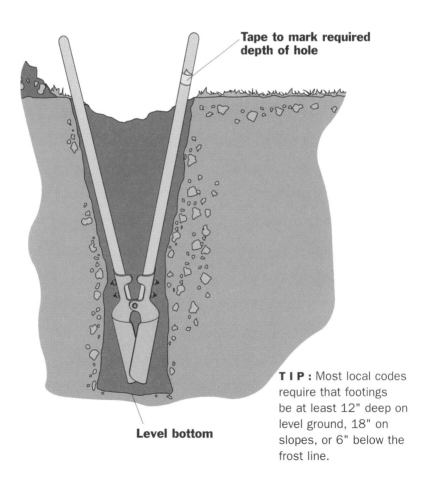

Tape to mark required depth of hole

Level bottom

TIP: Most local codes require that footings be at least 12" deep on level ground, 18" on slopes, or 6" below the frost line.

Build the forms

Place gravel in each hole. Cut lengths of forming tube so the bottoms are 8 to 12 inches above the hole bottoms and the tops are 8 inches above the ground. Set each tube in its hole, center it, and measure down from the string lines to level the top with the other tubes. Fasten two 2×4 cleats to the sides. Check the tube for plumb and brace it with a diagonal brace or scraps of wood wedged around it. Cut a length of rebar for each footing. Remove the string lines and call for inspection before pouring concrete.

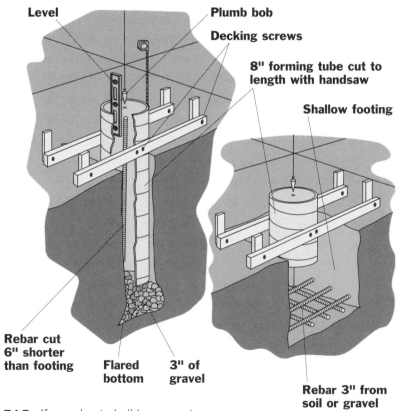

Level

Plumb bob

Decking screws

8" forming tube cut to length with handsaw

Shallow footing

Rebar cut 6" shorter than footing

Flared bottom

3" of gravel

Rebar 3" from soil or gravel

TIP: If you plan to build a concrete landing for stairs, form and pour it at the same time as the footings. See page 46.

4 Place the concrete

Pour concrete mix into a wheelbarrow or other strong, watertight container. Scoop a hole in the center, then add water gradually as you mix. Don't overdo it! Too much water weakens the concrete. (Use a bucket to monitor the amount of water rather than add it directly from a hose.) With a hoe, mix the ingredients thoroughly so the cement paste coats all of the aggregate. When properly mixed, the concrete will be wet enough to pour yet dry enough to hold its shape when you form it into small ridges.

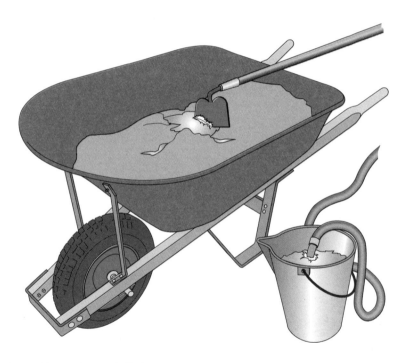

TIP: Concrete can irritate your skin, especially if you don't wash it away quickly. Wear gloves and long sleeves, and follow the manufacturer's recommendations.

Carefully place 1 or 2 feet of concrete in the forming tube and center the rebar in it. After the concrete stiffens slightly, pull the rebar up so the bottom is at least 3 inches above the soil or gravel, and the top is 2 inches below the top of the tube (to prevent rust). As you place the rest of the concrete, consolidate it by jabbing a long stick in the mix. Tap the outside of the form with a hammer to release air pockets, then level the top with a scrap of wood. Rinse the wheelbarrow and tools immediately.

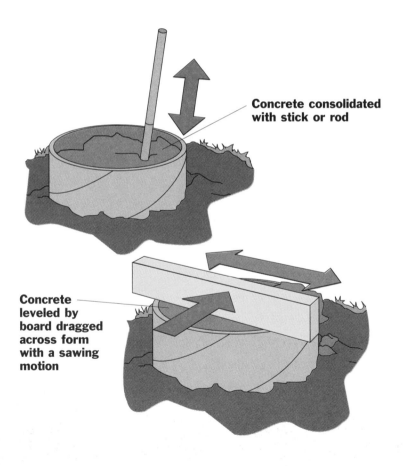

Concrete consolidated with stick or rod

Concrete leveled by board dragged across form with a sawing motion

Install post anchors

Before the concrete sets, reattach the strings and quickly recheck them for square. Holding a plumb bob or a chalk-line reel against the string lines, locate the post center on each footing and insert a J-bolt, nose first, into the concrete at that point. Wiggle the bolt into place so that the concrete settles around it. About an inch of bolt should stick out. Recheck its position with the plumb bob. Be sure to avoid splashing concrete on the threads.

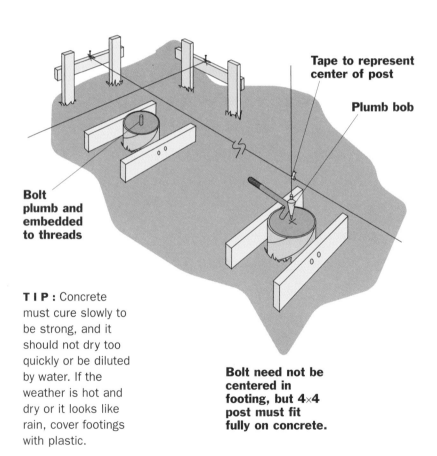

Tape to represent center of post

Plumb bob

Bolt plumb and embedded to threads

T I P : Concrete must cure slowly to be strong, and it should not dry too quickly or be diluted by water. If the weather is hot and dry or it looks like rain, cover footings with plastic.

Bolt need not be centered in footing, but 4×4 post must fit fully on concrete.

After the concrete hardens, place a metal post anchor over each bolt and install the washer and nut loosely. Lay a long, straight board against the anchors to align them. (It's easy to see if a piece of wood is straight—just sight down the length of it.) Double-check alignment by moving each string line 1¾ inches (half of a 4×4) outward and plumbing from the strings to the outside edges of the post anchors. Once they're aligned, tighten the nuts. Then dismantle the batter boards.

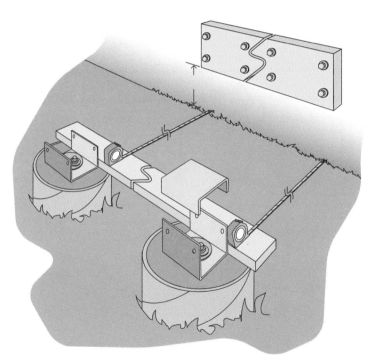

Aligning board parallel with ledger

1 Install the posts

With the string lines as a guide, measure and cut the posts so they will stand slightly taller than the ledger bottom. (You will trim them later.) For each post, make two stakes and have two boards handy for braces. Insert the post into the anchor and tack it in place temporarily with one 8-penny (8d) hot-dipped galvanized (HDG) nail. Make the post as straight as possible, but don't try to plumb it yet. On two sides of the post, attach braces with one screw each so that they will pivot. Drive stakes into the ground next to each brace.

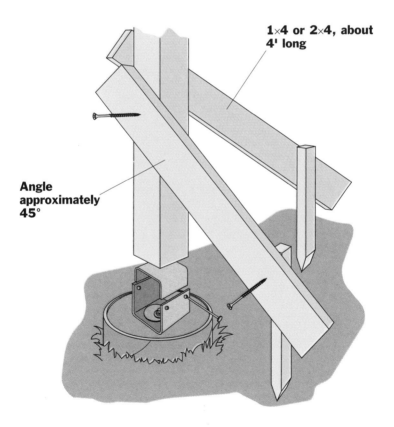

1×4 or 2×4, about 4' long

Angle approximately 45°

Plumb and mark posts

Holding a level against the post, plumb it and have a helper secure the brace to the stake with a screw. Then do the same with the other brace. Now recheck both sides for plumb. Adjust by relocating screws. When the post is plumb on both sides, drive additional screws into both the post and the stake. Fix the base in place by pounding one 8d HDG nail through each side of the anchor and into each side of the post. With a utility knife, cut away the section of forming tube

that shows above the ground. Rest one end of a long, straight board on top of the ledger.

Hold the other end against a corner post. Place a level on top of the board, level it, and mark where the bottom of the board touches the post. Then, using a scrap of joist lumber, measure down from that mark a distance equal to the joist depth and mark it. This indicates the top of the beam. Do the same for the other corner post. Mark the interior posts by holding a straight board or string line from corner post to corner post.

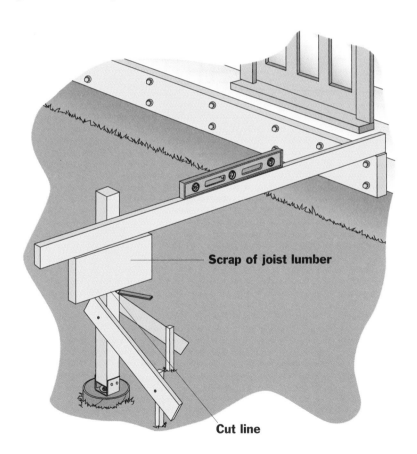

Scrap of joist lumber

Cut line

3 Install the beam

Carefully align the beam boards (or beam, if you use a 4-by) and fasten them in place temporarily with a decking screw at one end of each board and a nail partially driven into the post at the opposite end. (If the boards are bowed, you may have to bend them to get them to align exactly with the lines on each post.) Clamp the boards to the posts and drill two $\frac{1}{2}$-inch holes through the boards at each post. Then install $\frac{1}{2}$-inch by 8-inch carriage bolts with malleable washers.

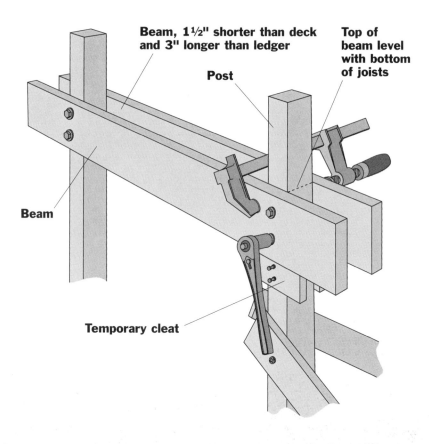

Beam, 1½" shorter than deck and 3" longer than ledger

Top of beam level with bottom of joists

Post

Beam

Temporary cleat

Trim the posts

Trim the post with a coarse-cut handsaw. Saw with easy strokes, letting the saw do the work. Wear eye protection, gloves, and, if working with pressure-treated lumber, a dust mask. (If you're comfortable using a reciprocating saw, this is an ideal time to put it to use.) Saturate the top of the post with wood sealer to guard against moisture damage.

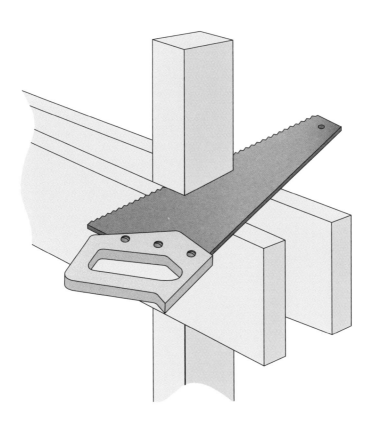

Install joists and header

Drill three ⅛-inch pilot holes into each side joist, ¾ inch from the ledger end. Rest the other end on the beam and hold the first end against the ledger so the tops are flush. Secure the joist to the ledger with 3-inch decking screws. Toenail the joist to the beam boards with 8d HDG common nails. The outside of each joist should be flush with the ends of the beam boards. Drill pilot holes into the header joist near each end and attach it to the side joists with 3-inch decking screws.

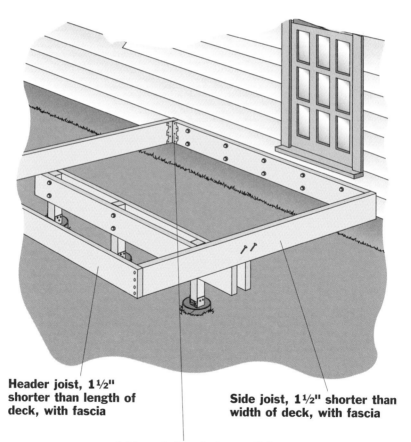

Header joist, 1½" shorter than length of deck, with fascia

Side joist, 1½" shorter than width of deck, with fascia

Add angle brackets on all four corners. Use joist-hanger nails.

Next, lay out the joist locations on the ledger and header.

Joist spacing can vary, but the most common is 16 inches on center. To mark the ledger, hook the tape measure to the outside of the side joist. Every 16 inches, make a mark and place a large *x* beside it. The *x* indicates the side of the mark on which the joist should be positioned. Use a try square or combination square to extend the mark. When marking the header joist, start at the same end as you did on the ledger.

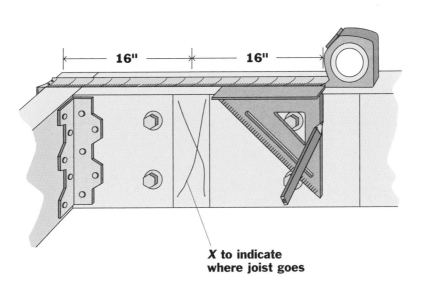

**X to indicate
where joist goes**

T I P : It is an easy mistake to place joists on the wrong side of the marks, causing them to be 1½" out of alignment. Double-check your layout.

Attach joist hangers

To attach joist hangers to the ledger, set each in position and nail only one side in place with two HDG joist-hanger nails. Make sure that the bottom of the hanger is flush with the bottom of the ledger. Then place a scrap of joist material into the hanger, bend the hanger into position, and nail the second side. At each step, use only two nails so you can make adjustments later, if necessary.

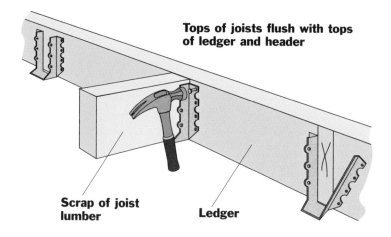

Tops of joists flush with tops of ledger and header

Scrap of joist lumber

Ledger

TIP: Lumber may vary in width. Check that the scrap you are using as a spacer is the same width as the joists.

7 Install the joists

Measure each joist and cut it to length. Both ends should be square and free of splits. Apply sealer to cut ends. Set each joist in place with the crown (high point) up. Make sure all joists are straight and parallel. Nail the joists to the joist hangers and complete the joist-hanger nailing. Facenail each joist to the header with three 16d HDG common nails. Toenail the joists to the beam. Install a row of blocking over the beam, measuring for each block at the header and ledger, and checking the alignment of joists as you install the blocks.

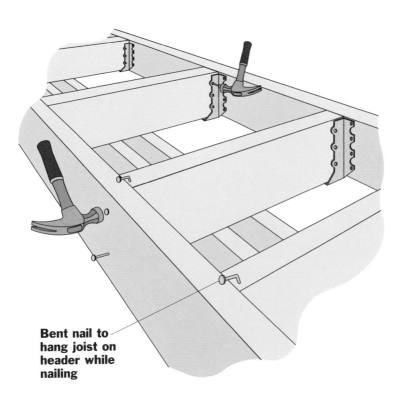

Bent nail to hang joist on header while nailing

Install starter board

Cut and install the fascia. Attach it with 8d HDG nails, two every 24 inches, or with 2-inch decking screws, driven from behind the joists. Lay a few 2-by decking boards across the joists for a working platform. Cut and place the first board along the house, leaving a ¼-inch gap. Its ends should be flush with the outside of the fascia. Stretch a string along its edge to make sure it is straight. Attach it with 3-inch decking screws or 12d HDG nails at each joist (use 8d nails for 1-by or ⁵⁄₄-inch decking).

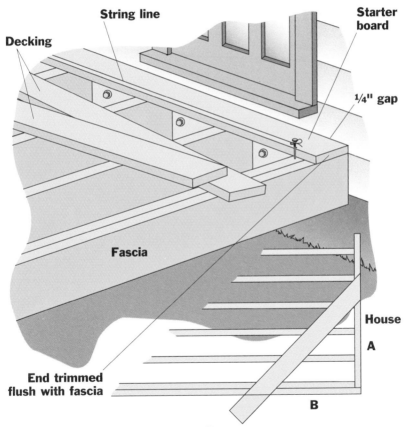

To install decking at a 45° angle, first cut one end of each board at 45°. Install the longest piece first so that distance A equals distance B.

2 Fasten the decking

Examine and sort the decking before laying it. Choose the best-looking side and cut off split or discolored ends. Install unattractive pieces in inconspicuous areas where you might eventually locate a bench, planter, or built-in table. Don't bother stopping to trim each end flush with the fascia—allow the decking to "run wild" (let it hang over the deck edge). You'll make a single finish cut later. Use 16d nails as spacers so you end up with uniform gaps between the decking boards.

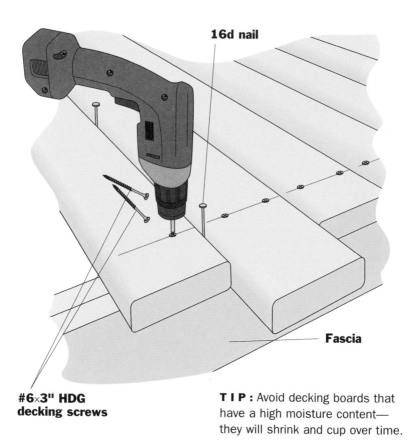

16d nail

Fascia

#6×3" HDG
decking screws

TIP: Avoid decking boards that have a high moisture content— they will shrink and cup over time.

Drive nails at a slight angle for better holding power. If you have difficulty driving screws straight, drill pilot holes. Whether using nails or screws, drill pilot holes at ends of boards to prevent splits. Where boards join end-to-end, set the nails or screws back from the joint and drive them at an angle into the joist. Avoid placing joints next to each other—it is unsightly and will weaken the deck. Instead, stagger joints by at least two joists.

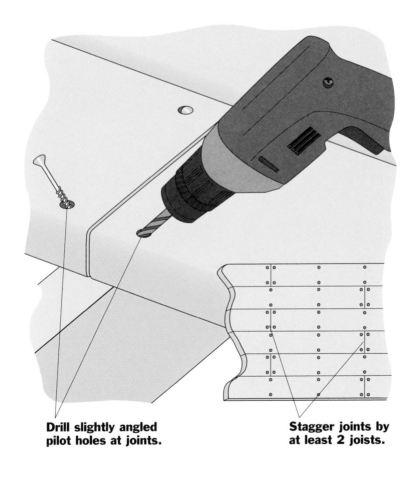

Drill slightly angled pilot holes at joints.

Stagger joints by at least 2 joists.

Straighten as you go

Straighten warped boards as you fasten them. Test the decking for straightness every fourth piece or so, using a string line as you did with the starter board. When you're halfway across, measure at several points to see if the decking is parallel with the header. If not, make adjustments a little at a time, over several boards, rather than all at once. At the same time, estimate how wide the last piece of decking will be and, if necessary, adjust the gaps slightly to prevent ending up with a narrow board for the last piece.

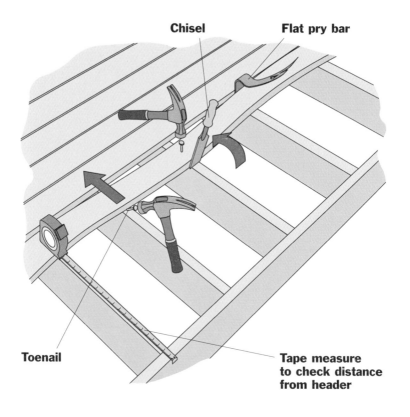

Chisel

Flat pry bar

Toenail

Tape measure to check distance from header

Make the finish cuts

Snap a chalk line directly above the outside edge of the fascia. Set the blade of the circular saw so that it will cut no more than ⅛ inch below the decking. Clear the area of any obstructions so you can concentrate on the task. While cutting, try not to constantly make small adjustments. Instead, cut freely. (If you are nervous about cutting a straight line, practice on some scrap lumber first, or tack a long, straight board on the decking as a saw guide.)

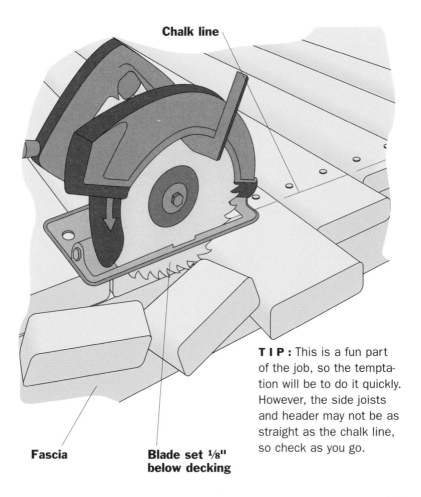

Chalk line

Fascia

Blade set ⅛"
below decking

TIP: This is a fun part of the job, so the temptation will be to do it quickly. However, the side joists and header may not be as straight as the chalk line, so check as you go.

Adding Stairs and Railings

Figure the stair layout

Measure the total rise from deck surface to landing. Divide this distance by 7½ inches (the maximum riser height). Round the answer up to the next whole number; this is the number of risers. Divide that number back into the total rise to get the exact height of each riser. For example, a total rise of 35⅝ inches would require five 7⅛-inch risers and four runs, or steps (the deck is the final step). Since each run is 11 inches (two 2×6s), the total run, or stairway length, is 44 inches.

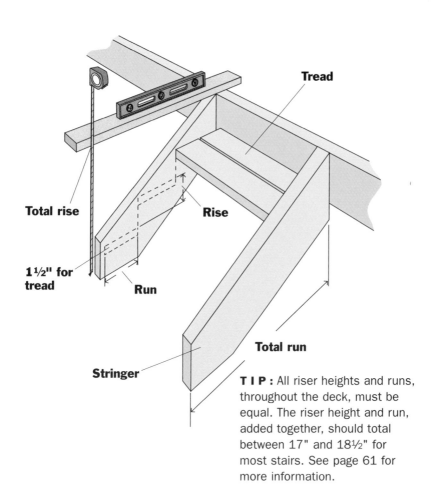

Tread

Total rise

Rise

1½" for tread

Run

Total run

Stringer

TIP: All riser heights and runs, throughout the deck, must be equal. The riser height and run, added together, should total between 17" and 18½" for most stairs. See page 61 for more information.

2 Build the stair landing

Excavate and build forms for a 4-inch concrete pad with a 4-inch bed of tamped gravel. Cut and place reinforcing mesh on the gravel. Mix and place the concrete, centering the mesh in the concrete. Screed the surface with a straight 2×4, then smooth it with a wood float. Run a pointed trowel between the concrete and form boards; follow with an edger. Insert anchor bolts for the posts, approximately 18 inches back from the front edge of the stairs. After an hour or so, smooth the concrete with a steel trowel.

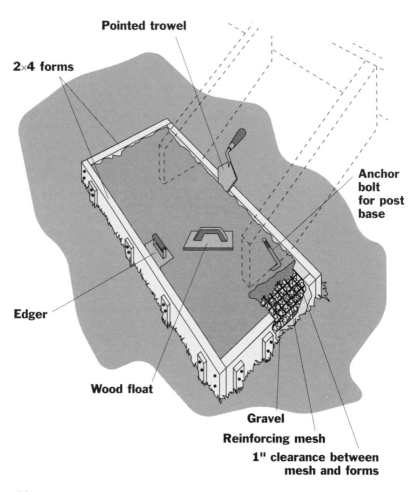

Pointed trowel

2×4 forms

Anchor bolt for post base

Edger

Wood float

Gravel

Reinforcing mesh

1" clearance between mesh and forms

Lay out and cut stringers

Lay a framing square on a 2×12 so that the rise and run dimensions intersect the board's edge. Mark an outline of the square. Slide the square to the next position and scribe another outline. Repeat this process for each step. Draw lines for the tread bottoms as well as cut lines at the ends of the stringer.

Lay out the second stringer the same way, double-checking all measurements. Cut out the first stringer, check it for fit, then cut out the second. Predrill and attach tread cleats with lag screws (don't drill through the board).

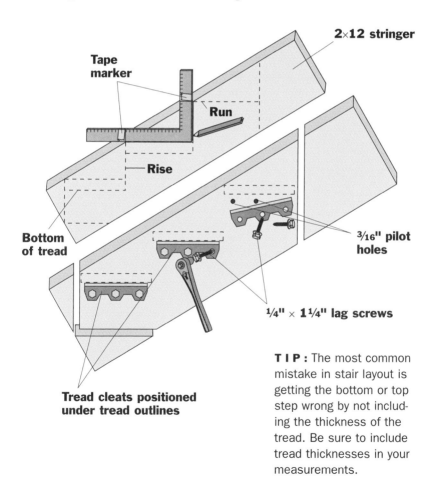

2×12 stringer

Tape marker

Run

Rise

Bottom of tread

³⁄₁₆" pilot holes

¼" × 1¼" lag screws

Tread cleats positioned under tread outlines

TIP: The most common mistake in stair layout is getting the bottom or top step wrong by not including the thickness of the tread. Be sure to include tread thicknesses in your measurements.

47

Install stringers; treads

Tack the stringers in place temporarily with nails driven through the joist and partially into the back of the stringers. Cut 2×6 treads and lay them on top of the cleats. Check them for level, and square the stringers to the deck. After rechecking all measurements, finish driving the nails into the stringers.

Install angle brackets where the stringers connect to the joist; attach them with 1¼-inch decking screws or 16d HDG joist-hanger nails. Attach the treads from below with ¼-inch by 1¼-inch lag screws; predrill, but not through the treads.

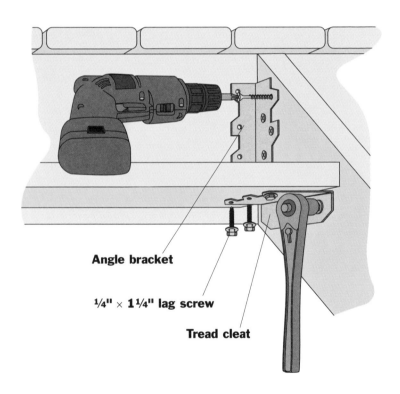

Angle bracket

¼" × 1¼" lag screw

Tread cleat

Install stair-railing posts

Cut the posts longer than needed. You will mark the angle and trim them later. Install and adjust the post anchors so they are in line with the stringers, and tighten them in place. Fasten each post to its anchor with 16d HDG joist-hanger nails. Plumb the posts and tack or clamp them to the stringers. Drill two ⅜-inch pilot holes through each stringer and post, then insert ⅜-inch by 6-inch carriage bolts from the post side and install washers and nuts. Hacksaw the protruding bolts flush with the nuts.

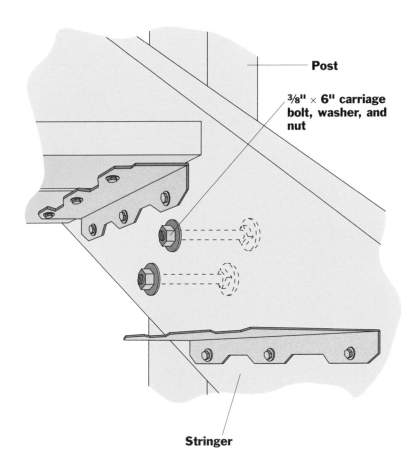

Post

⅜" × 6" carriage bolt, washer, and nut

Stringer

6 Install deck-railing posts

Cut the railing posts to length (bottom of fascia to bottom of cap rail, which is 1½ inches below final railing height). You will need two railing posts where the stairway meets the deck, two for each outside corner, and one every 4 to 6 feet in between. Space them evenly for a pleasing appearance. Many people choose to cut the bottoms of posts and balusters at a 30- or 45-degree angle.

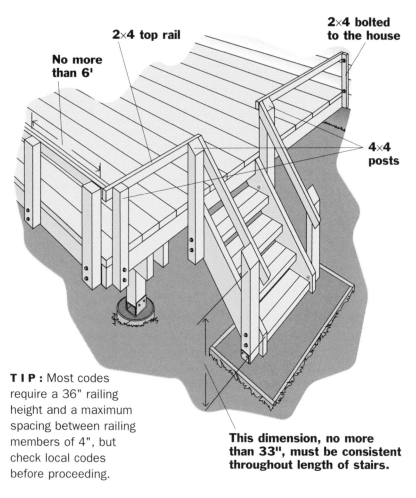

2×4 bolted to the house

2×4 top rail

No more than 6'

4×4 posts

TIP: Most codes require a 36" railing height and a maximum spacing between railing members of 4", but check local codes before proceeding.

This dimension, no more than 33", must be consistent throughout length of stairs.

Attach the posts with ⅜-inch by 6-inch carriage bolts with washers and nuts. Check for plumb as you go. Install 2×4 top rails flush with the tops of the posts. Attach them with 3-inch decking screws; drill pilot holes at the ends of the boards. Install the stair railings last. To mark the posts for cutting, hold or tack the rails in place, parallel with the stringer. Hold a level at the end of the rails to mark a plumb cut line, 6 inches from the post (some codes require that the railing terminate at a post).

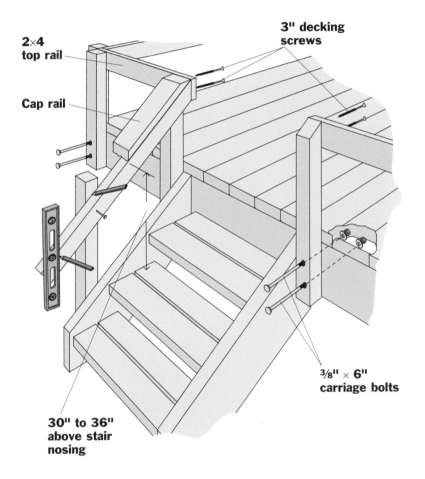

3" decking screws

2×4 top rail

Cap rail

³⁄₈" × 6" carriage bolts

30" to 36" above stair nosing

Install the cap rail

Make the cap rail out of the same material as the decking. Choose straight pieces, as free of knots as possible. Fasten them with two screws at each post, and one screw every foot or so along the rail. Miter the corner joints, cutting each piece at 45 degrees. Locate other joints over the middle of posts.

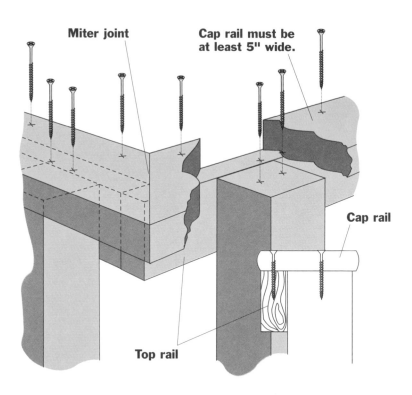

Miter joint

Cap rail must be at least 5" wide.

Cap rail

Top rail

To make a tight-fitting miter joint, cut the first board at 45 degrees, to exact length, and install it. Then lay the second board in place, scribe the bottom of it where the first board intersects, and cut along the mark. When you can, let boards run wild as you did with the decking. That way, if you make a mistake, you will have extra length for recutting. After installing the railings, use a wood file, sanding block, or belt sander to round off any edges people are likely to bump into—especially near the stairway.

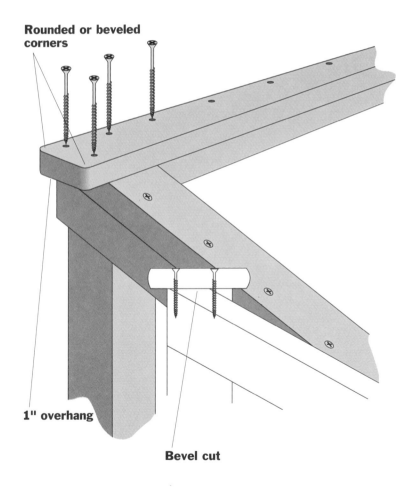

Rounded or beveled corners

1" overhang

Bevel cut

Install the balusters

Cut the balusters the same length as the posts. Drill four ⅛-inch pilot holes into each, two at the bottom and two at the top. Determine the spacing between balusters—for most codes the maximum is 4 inches—and cut a spacer to that width. Position the first baluster and drive in one screw at the fascia. Plumb the baluster and drive in the remaining screws. Use the spacer to position the balusters, top and bottom, checking for plumb every fourth baluster. For the stair railings, cut balusters at the same angle as the stair-railing posts.

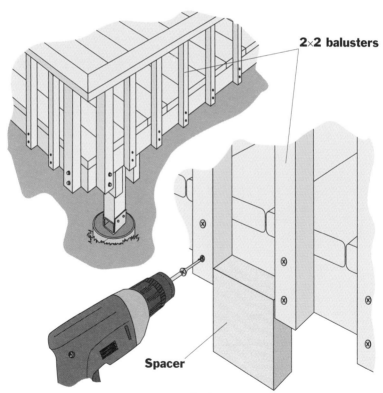

2×2 balusters

Spacer

TIP: Railings involve repetitive cutting of short pieces. A chop saw (power miter saw) makes the job much easier, especially for angled cuts. Consider renting one.

The railing system is the most visible part of the deck, so plan it carefully. How will it look against the house? Does it complement the style of your home? The railing system shown in the previous steps is used widely throughout the country. However, by combining 2×2s, 2×4s, and 2×6s in other ways, you can develop your own railing design in keeping with the architectural style of your home.

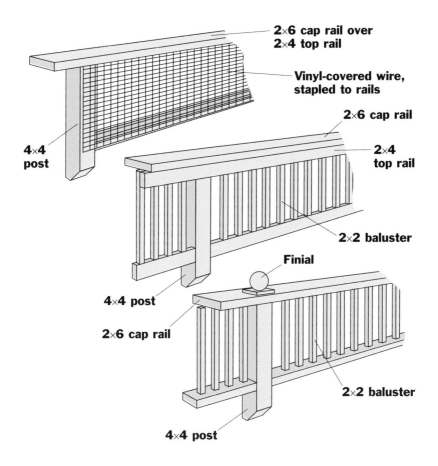

2×6 cap rail over
2×4 top rail

Vinyl-covered wire,
stapled to rails

2×6 cap rail

2×4
top rail

4×4
post

2×2 baluster

Finial

4×4 post

2×6 cap rail

2×2 baluster

4×4 post

Sealers and Stains

No deck finish is perfect. All need to be reapplied from time to time, and none solves every potential problem. You can choose "clear" finishes (some of which actually have some pigment in them, and so are not really clear), semitransparent stains, or solid-color finishes, according to what looks best to you. But make sure that you get the type of protection you need. A good finish will contain at least some of the following ingredients.

Ingredient	Description	When to Use
Water repellent	Usually made of paraffin, it keeps water from soaking in.	Essential for cut ends of boards. Causes water to bead on surface of the wood, not soak in.
Preservatives	Includes fungicide, mildewcide, and insecticide in various combinations.	Varies to meet local conditions.
UV blockers	Usually a pigment that protects from the sun's ultraviolet rays, keeping wood from turning gray. Because it has color added, it compromises the original color of the wood.	Use if the deck is in direct sunlight and you want to keep it from turning gray.
Resins and oils	Often made with linseed oil or alkyd resins, these finishes will harden and yellow, giving the deck a glossy appearance.	Use if you like the "wet" look for wood.

Fastening Hardware

Decks are exposed constantly to the weather. All hardware must be corrosion-resistant. In addition, the right hardware will speed the job and strengthen the deck substantially. Here are the fasteners most commonly used for deck building.

Framing Connectors

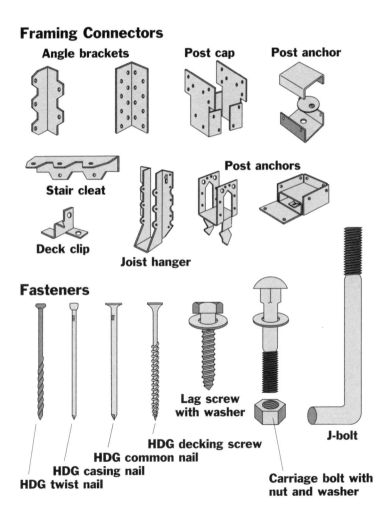

Angle brackets

Post cap

Post anchor

Stair cleat

Post anchors

Deck clip

Joist hanger

Fasteners

Lag screw with washer

J-bolt

HDG decking screw

HDG common nail

HDG casing nail

HDG twist nail

Carriage bolt with nut and washer

Lumber Dimensions

Actual dimensions of lumber differ from their nominal dimensions—the names by which they are identified. This can cause confusion in drawing plans and estimating materials. Here are the nominal and actual dimensions of lumber commonly used in building decks.

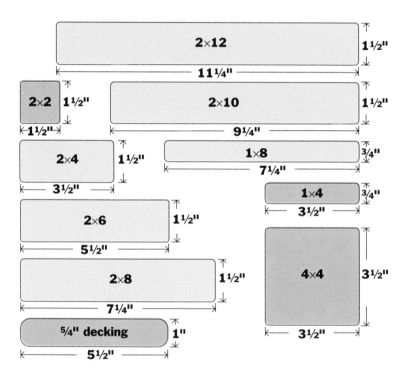

TIP: Heartwood or sapwood? Especially for redwood but also for cedar, the heartwood, taken from the center of the log, is more resistant to weather and insects than the lighter-colored sapwood.

Types of Deck Lumber

Here's what you get for your money when you select various types of lumber. Among these options, the prettier woods also tend to last longer. Don't be tempted to build a deck with untreated pine or fir, however. Both types will begin to rot within a few years.

Woods Used for Decking

Type	Advantages	Drawbacks
Pressure-treated: Pine or Douglas fir	Lasts much longer than redwood or cedar. It is usually the cheapest and strongest—use it for posts, beams, and joists.	Has a tendency to split and splinter; has varied grain and color. Tends to have high moisture content. Must be handled and disposed of with care due to toxicity of preservative.
Cedar	Attractive appearance. Resists splintering and shrinking. Usually less expensive than redwood.	Will gray if left untreated. If subject to standing moisture, can begin to rot within five years. The softest and least strong of *these three*.
Redwood	Attractive appearance. Resists shrinking and warping. Easy to work with. Resists rot better than cedar, though not as well as pressure treated. Is stronger than cedar and can be used for posts or joists.	Expensive. Splits more readily than cedar.
Tropical hard-woods	Durable and very strong. Usually free of knots, with straight grain.	Expensive. Heavy. May be hard to find, especially from sources that harvest trees from sustained-growth forests.
Synthetic lumber	Made from recycled plastics. Extremely durable. Easy to paint or stain. No knots or warping. Good for decks.	Heavy. Price equivalent to better grades of redwood. Limited sizes and lengths.

Inspecting Lumber

Instead of just having the lumberyard select and deliver all the material, take some time to inspect and choose your lumber. Don't try to get all perfect wood, but eliminate truly bad boards. Here are some defects to look out for.

How Types of Pressure-Treated Lumber Compare

Species	Advantages	Disadvantages
Southern pine	Strong and hard. Absorbs preservative readily, so resists rotting the best.	Prone to warping, splitting, and splintering.
Douglas fir	Resists warping and splitting.	Resists preservative (thus you often see incisions used to inject it) and is therefore more prone to rotting and insects.
Hem-fir	Inexpensive.	Weakest of the three. Prone to splitting and warping.

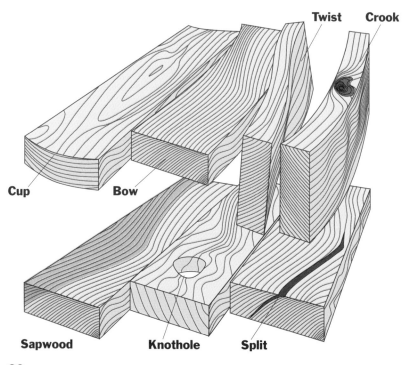

Twist   Crook

Cup   Bow

Sapwood   Knothole   Split

Stair Dimensions

The usual riser for stairs is around 7½ inches, but for porches and decks some people prefer a more gentle slope, with 6-inch risers or even less. Deep treads, combined with wide stairways, can also double as overflow seating for parties or provide a tiered area for potted plants. Below are some comfortable combinations of risers and treads that can fit a variety of situations.

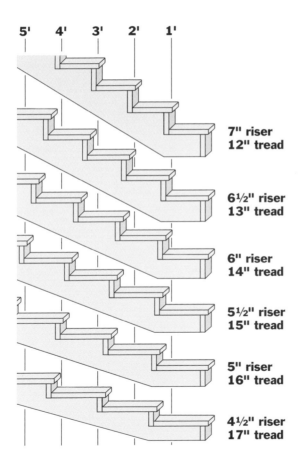

5' 4' 3' 2' 1'

**7" riser
12" tread**

**6½" riser
13" tread**

**6" riser
14" tread**

**5½" riser
15" tread**

**5" riser
16" tread**

**4½" riser
17" tread**

Lumber Spans

Use span tables to determine maximum spans for specific sizes of lumber, or what size lumber you need for a given span. The two charts below will help you plan your deck. Use the Recommended Maximum Spans for Decking Boards chart to see how closely joists must be spaced to support the decking you plan to use; then use the Maximum Joist Spans table to determine the size joists you will need for the span between the ledger and beam. Whenever possible, use the next-larger size of lumber—decks should be designed for parties where many people congregate.

Recommended Maximum Spans for Decking Boards*

	Species Group		
	A	B	C
Laid Flat**			
Nominal 1" boards	16"	14"	12"
5/4" pressure-treated boards	24"	16"	—
Nominal 2×3	28"	24"	20"
Nominal 2×4	32"	28"	20"
Nominal 2×6	42"	36"	28"
Laid on Edge			
2×3	48"	40"	32"
2×4	72"	60"	48"

*Spans are based on the use of construction-grade lumber or better (select structural, appearance, No. 1, or No. 2).

**These spans are based on the assumption that more than one floorboard carries normal loads. If concentrated loads are a rule, reduce spans accordingly.

Maximum Joist Spans (beam spacing)*

Joist Size	Species Group		
	A	B	C
12" Joist Spacing			
2×6	10' 6"	10' 0"	9' 0"
2×8	14' 0"	12' 6"	11' 0"
2×10	17' 6"	15' 8"	13' 10"
2×12	21' 0"	19' 4"	17' 6"
16" Joist Spacing			
2×6	9' 7"	8' 6"	7' 7"
2×8	12' 6"	11' 0"	10' 0"
2×10	16' 2"	14' 4"	13' 0"
2×12	19' 0"	18' 6"	16' 0"
24" Joist Spacing			
2×6	8' 6"	7' 4"	6' 8"
2×8	11' 2"	9' 9"	8' 7"
2×10	14' 0"	12' 6"	11' 0"
2×12	16' 6"	16' 0"	13' 6"
32" Joist Spacing			
2×6	7' 6"	6' 9"	6' 0"
2×8	10' 0"	9' 1"	8' 2"
2×10	12' 10"	11' 8"	10' 8"
2×12	14' 6"	14' 0"	12' 6"

*Joists are on edge. Spans are center-to-center distances between beams or ledger and beam. Loads are based on 40 psf deck live load plus 10 psf dead load. Assumes a grade equivalent to #2 or better (#2 medium-grain southern pine).

U.S./Metric Measure Conversions

Formulas for Exact Measures

	Symbol	When you know:	Multiply by:	To find:
Mass (Weight)	oz	ounces	28.35	grams
	lb	pounds	0.45	kilograms
	g	grams	0.035	ounces
	kg	kilograms	2.2	pounds
Volume	pt	pints	0.47	liters
	qt	quarts	0.95	liters
	gal	gallons	3.785	liters
	ml	milliliters	0.034	fluid ounces
Length	in.	inches	2.54	centimeters
	ft	feet	30.48	centimeters
	yd	yards	0.9144	meters
	mi	miles	1.609	kilometers
	km	kilometers	0.621	miles
	m	meters	1.094	yards
	cm	centimeters	0.39	inches
Temperature	°F	Fahrenheit	$5/9$ (after subtracting 32)	Celsius
	°C	Celsius	$9/5$ (then add 32)	Fahrenheit
Area	in.^{2}	square inches	6.452	square centimeters
	ft^2	square feet	929.0	square centimeters
	yd^2	square yards	8361.0	square centimeters
	a.	acres	0.4047	hectares

Rounded Measures for Quick Reference

1 oz		= 30 g
4 oz		= 115 g
8 oz		= 225 g
16 oz	= 1 lb	= 450 g
32 oz	= 2 lb	= 900 g
36 oz	= $2^1/_4$ lb	= 1000 g (1 kg)
1 c	= 8 oz	= 250 ml
2 c (1pt)	= 16 oz	= 500 ml
4 c (1 qt)	= 32 oz	= 1 liter
4 qt (1 gal)	= 128 oz	= $3^3/_4$ liter
$3/_8$ in.		= 1.0 cm
1 in.		= 2.5 cm
2 in.		= 5.0 cm
$2^1/_2$ in.		= 6.5 cm
12 in. (1 ft)		= 30.0 cm
1 yd		= 90.0 cm
100 ft		= 30.0 m
1 mi		= 1.6 km
32° F		= 0° C
212° F		= 100° C
1 in.^{2}		= 6.5 cm^2
1 ft^2		= 930 cm^2
1 yd^2		= 8360 cm^2
1 a.		= 4050 m^2